This book belongs to

: _____

My Phone Number: _____

Teacher's Name: _____

Teacher's Contact: _____

"To study music, we must learn the rules. To create music, we must break them."

- Nadia Boulanger

Circle of Fifths

Glossary

Write down the musical terms you have learned.

f	forte	Play loud!

Glossary (continued)

Write down the musical terms you have learned.

Glossary (continued)

Write down the musical terms you have learned.

Glossary (continued)

Write down the musical terms you have learned.

Glossary (continued)

Write down the musical terms you have learned.

Glossary (continued)

Write down the musical terms you have learned.

Date: _____

Technique/Exercises:

⭐

Repertoire:

Special Notes:

Practice Time Tracker:

Date:							
Minutes							
Initials:							

I have questions for the next lesson!

Date: _____

Technique/Exercises:

Repertoire:

Special Notes:

Practice Time Tracker:

Date:							
Minutes							
Initials:							

I have questions for the next lesson!

Date: _____

Technique/Exercises:

Repertoire:

Special Notes:

Practice Time Tracker:

Date:							
Minutes							
Initials:							

I have questions for the next lesson!

Date: _____

Technique/Exercises:

⭐

Repertoire:

Special Notes:

Practice Time Tracker:

Date:							
Minutes							
Initials:							

I have questions for the next lesson!

Date: _____

Technique/Exercises:

Repertoire:

Special Notes:

Practice Time Tracker:

Date:							
Minutes							
Initials:							

I have questions for the next lesson!

Date: _____

Technique/Exercises:

Repertoire:

Special Notes:

Practice Time Tracker:

Date:							
Minutes							
Initials:							

I have questions for the next lesson!

Date: _____

Technique/Exercises:

Repertoire:

Special Notes:

Practice Time Tracker:

Date:							
Minutes							
Initials:							

I have questions for the next lesson!

Date: _____

Technique/Exercises:

Repertoire:

Special Notes:

Practice Time Tracker:

Date:							
Minutes							
Initials:							

I have questions for the next lesson!

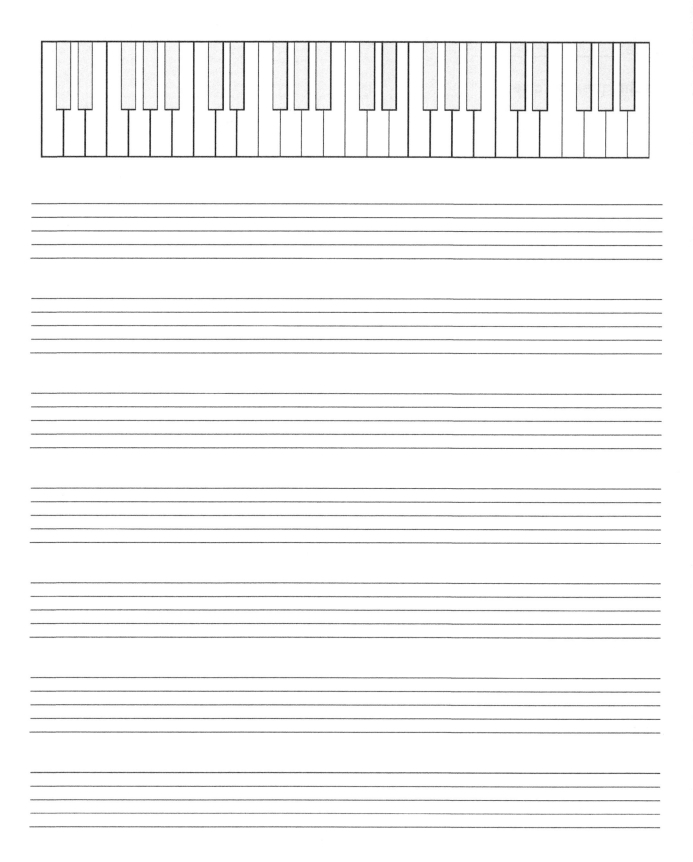

Date: _____

Technique/Exercises:

Repertoire:

Special Notes:

Practice Time Tracker:

Date:							
Minutes							
Initials:							

I have questions for the next lesson!

Date: _____

Technique/Exercises:

Repertoire:

Special Notes:

Practice Time Tracker:

Date:							
Minutes							
Initials:							

I have questions for the next lesson!

Date: _____

Technique/Exercises:

Repertoire:

Special Notes:

Practice Time Tracker:

Date:							
Minutes							
Initials:							

I have questions for the next lesson!

Date: _____

Technique/Exercises:

Repertoire:

Special Notes:

Practice Time Tracker:

Date:							
Minutes							
Initials:							

I have questions for the next lesson!

Date: _____

Technique/Exercises:

Repertoire:

Special Notes:

Practice Time Tracker:

Date:							
Minutes							
Initials:							

I have questions for the next lesson!

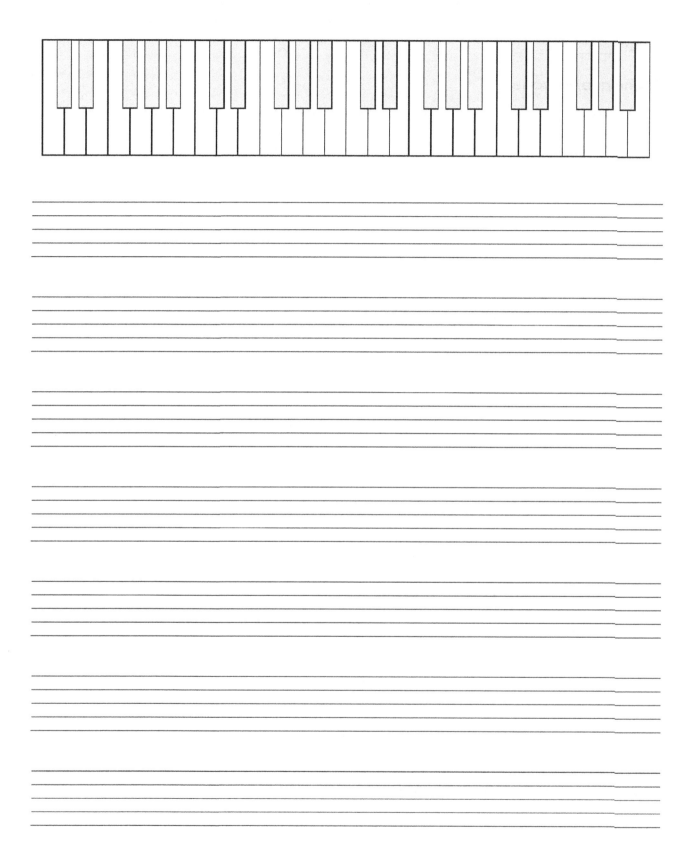

Date: _____

Technique/Exercises:

Repertoire:

Special Notes:

Practice Time Tracker:

Date:							
Minutes							
Initials:							

I have questions for the next lesson!

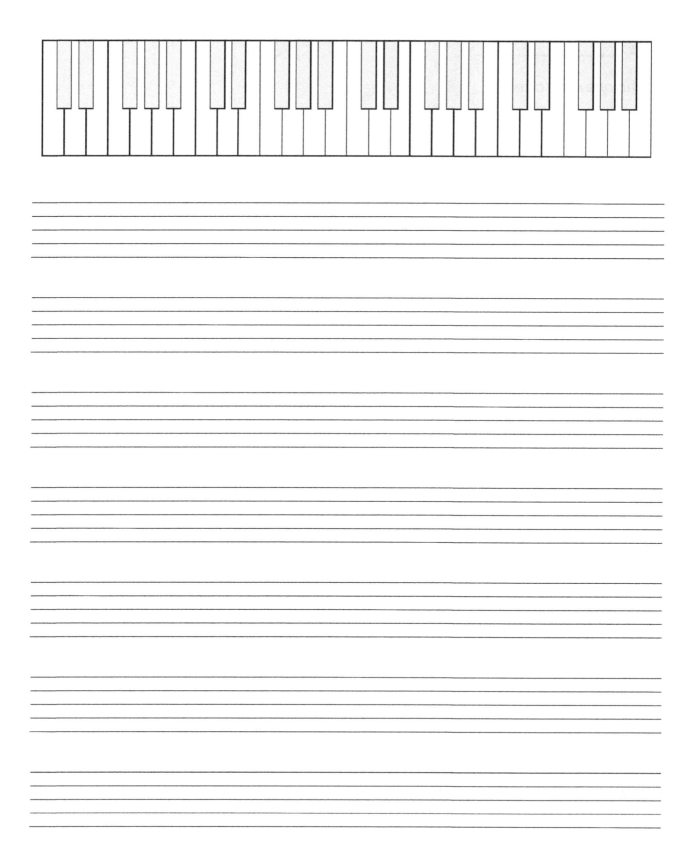

Date: _____

Technique/Exercises:

Repertoire:

Special Notes:

Practice Time Tracker:

Date:							
Minutes							
Initials:							

I have questions for the next lesson!

Date: _____

Technique/Exercises:

Repertoire:

Special Notes:

Practice Time Tracker:

Date:							
Minutes							
Initials:							

I have questions for the next lesson!

Date: _____

Technique/Exercises:

Repertoire:

Special Notes:

Practice Time Tracker:

Date:							
Minutes							
Initials:							

I have questions for the next lesson!

Date: _____

Technique/Exercises:

Repertoire:

Special Notes:

Practice Time Tracker:

Date:							
Minutes							
Initials:							

I have questions for the next lesson!

Date: _____

Technique/Exercises:

Repertoire:

Special Notes:

Practice Time Tracker:

Date:							
Minutes							
Initials:							

I have questions for the next lesson!

Date: _____

Technique/Exercises:

Repertoire:

Special Notes:

Practice Time Tracker:

Date:							
Minutes							
Initials:							

I have questions for the next lesson!

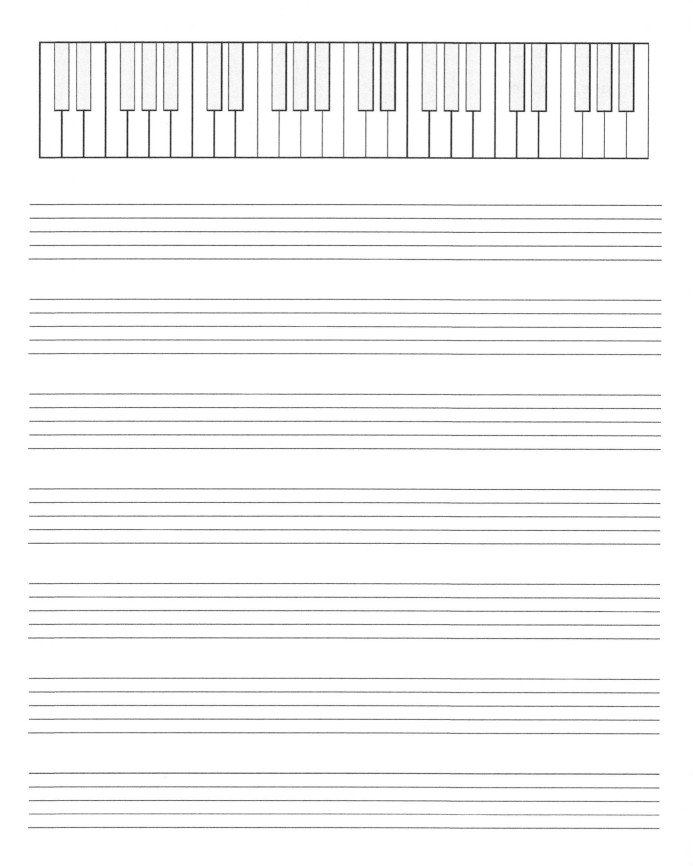

Date: _____

Technique/Exercises:

Repertoire:

Special Notes:

Practice Time Tracker:

Date:							
Minutes							
Initials:							

I have questions for the next lesson!

Date: _____

Technique/Exercises:

Repertoire:

Special Notes:

Practice Time Tracker:

Date:							
Minutes							
Initials:							

I have questions for the next lesson!

Date: _____

Technique/Exercises:

Repertoire:

Special Notes:

Practice Time Tracker:

Date:							
Minutes							
Initials:							

I have questions for the next lesson!

Date: _____

Technique/Exercises:

☆

Repertoire:

Special Notes:

Practice Time Tracker:

Date:							
Minutes							
Initials:							

I have questions for the next lesson!

Date: _____

Technique/Exercises:

Repertoire:

Special Notes:

Practice Time Tracker:

Date:							
Minutes							
Initials:							

I have questions for the next lesson!

Date: _____

Technique/Exercises:

Repertoire:

Special Notes:

Practice Time Tracker:

Date:							
Minutes							
Initials:							

I have questions for the next lesson!

Date: _____

Technique/Exercises:

Repertoire:

Special Notes:

Practice Time Tracker:

Date:							
Minutes							
Initials:							

I have questions for the next lesson!

Date: _____

Technique/Exercises:

Repertoire:

Special Notes:

Practice Time Tracker:

Date:							
Minutes							
Initials:							

I have questions for the next lesson!

Date: _____

Technique/Exercises:

Repertoire:

Special Notes:

Practice Time Tracker:

Date:							
Minutes							
Initials:							

I have questions for the next lesson!

Date: _____

Technique/Exercises:

Repertoire:

Special Notes:

Practice Time Tracker:

Date:							
Minutes							
Initials:							

I have questions for the next lesson!

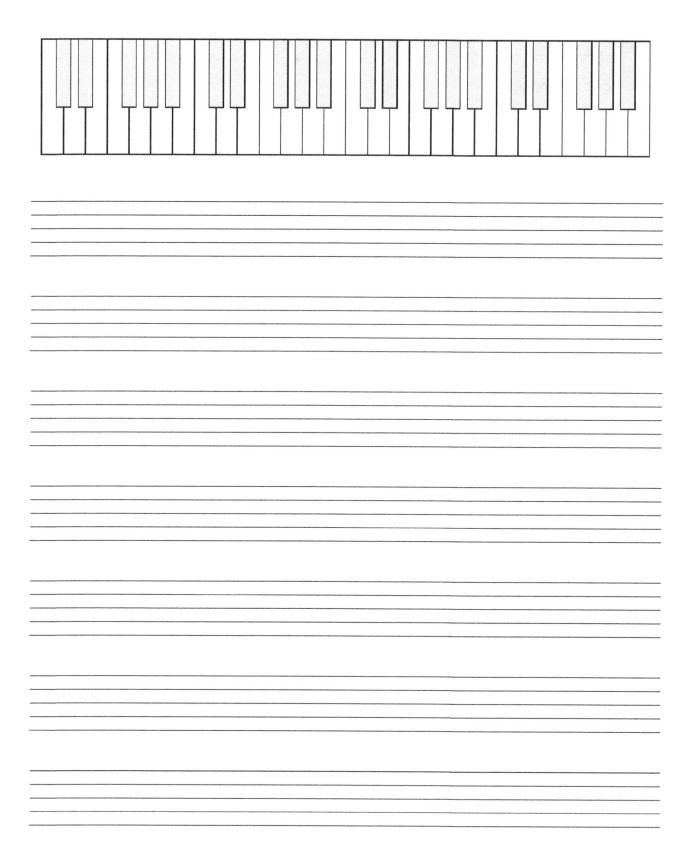

Date: _____

Technique/Exercises:

Repertoire:

Special Notes:

Practice Time Tracker:

Date:							
Minutes							
Initials:							

I have questions for the next lesson!

Date: _____

Technique/Exercises:

Repertoire:

Special Notes:

Practice Time Tracker:

Date:							
Minutes							
Initials:							

I have questions for the next lesson!

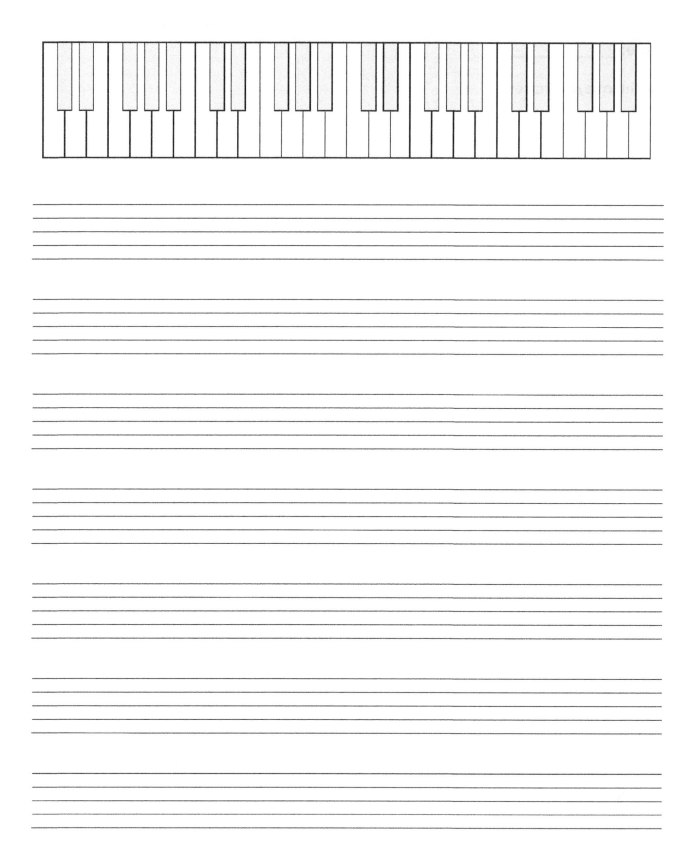

Date: _____

Technique/Exercises:

Repertoire:

Special Notes:

Practice Time Tracker:

Date:							
Minutes							
Initials:							

I have questions for the next lesson!

Date: _____

Technique/Exercises:

Repertoire:

Special Notes:

Practice Time Tracker:

Date:							
Minutes							
Initials:							

I have questions for the next lesson!

Date: _____

Technique/Exercises:

☆

Repertoire:

Special Notes:

Practice Time Tracker:

Date:							
Minutes							
Initials:							

I have questions for the next lesson!

Date: _____

Technique/Exercises:

Repertoire:

Special Notes:

Practice Time Tracker:

Date:							
Minutes							
Initials:							

I have questions for the next lesson!

Date: _____

Technique/Exercises:

Repertoire:

Special Notes:

Practice Time Tracker:

Date:							
Minutes							
Initials:							

I have questions for the next lesson!

Date: _____

Technique/Exercises:

Repertoire:

Special Notes:

Practice Time Tracker:

Date:							
Minutes							
Initials:							

I have questions for the next lesson!

Date: _____

Technique/Exercises:

Repertoire:

Special Notes:

Practice Time Tracker:

Date:							
Minutes							
Initials:							

I have questions for the next lesson!

Date: _____

Technique/Exercises:

Repertoire:

Special Notes:

Practice Time Tracker:

Date:							
Minutes							
Initials:							

I have questions for the next lesson!

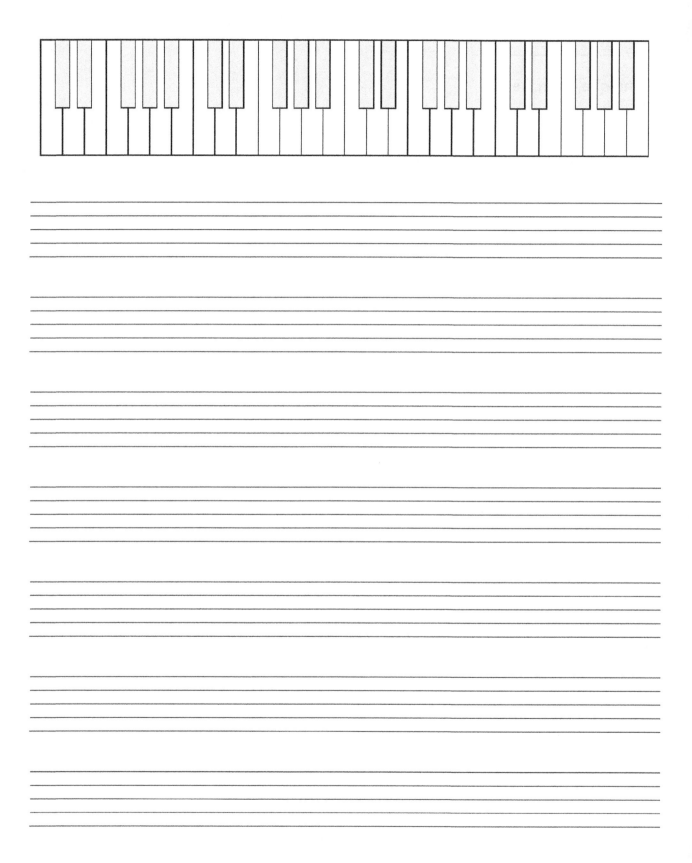

Date: _____

Technique/Exercises:

Repertoire:

Special Notes:

Practice Time Tracker:

Date:							
Minutes							
Initials:							

I have questions for the next lesson!

Date: _____

Technique/Exercises:

Repertoire:

Special Notes:

Practice Time Tracker:

Date:							
Minutes							
Initials:							

I have questions for the next lesson!

Date: _____

Technique/Exercises:

Repertoire:

Special Notes:

Practice Time Tracker:

Date:							
Minutes							
Initials:							

I have questions for the next lesson!

Date: _____

Technique/Exercises:

Repertoire:

Special Notes:

Practice Time Tracker:

Date:							
Minutes							
Initials:							

I have questions for the next lesson!

Date: _____

Technique/Exercises:

Repertoire:

Special Notes:

Practice Time Tracker:

Date:							
Minutes							
Initials:							

I have questions for the next lesson!

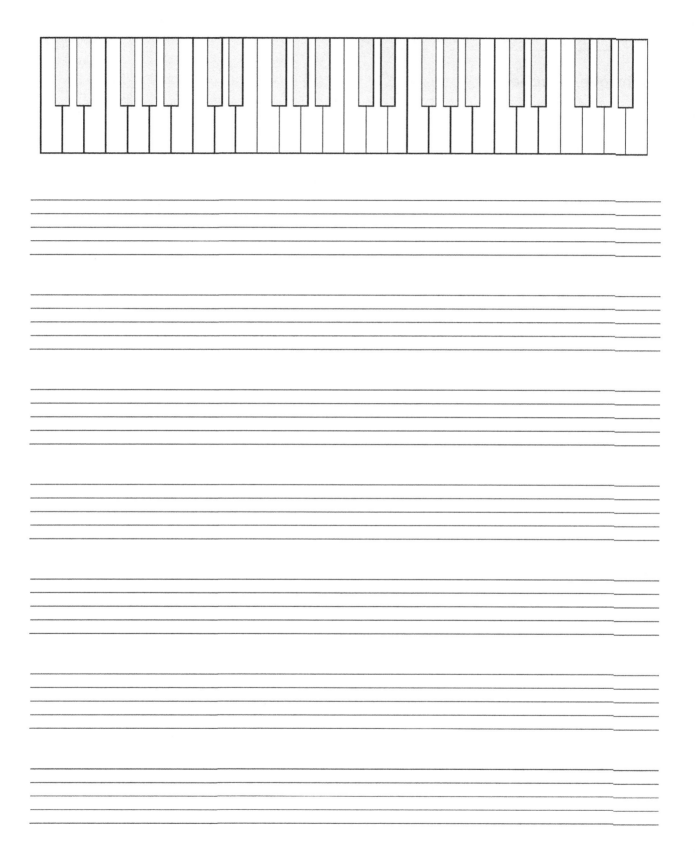

Date: _____

Technique/Exercises:

Repertoire:

Special Notes:

Practice Time Tracker:

Date:							
Minutes							
Initials:							

I have questions for the next lesson!

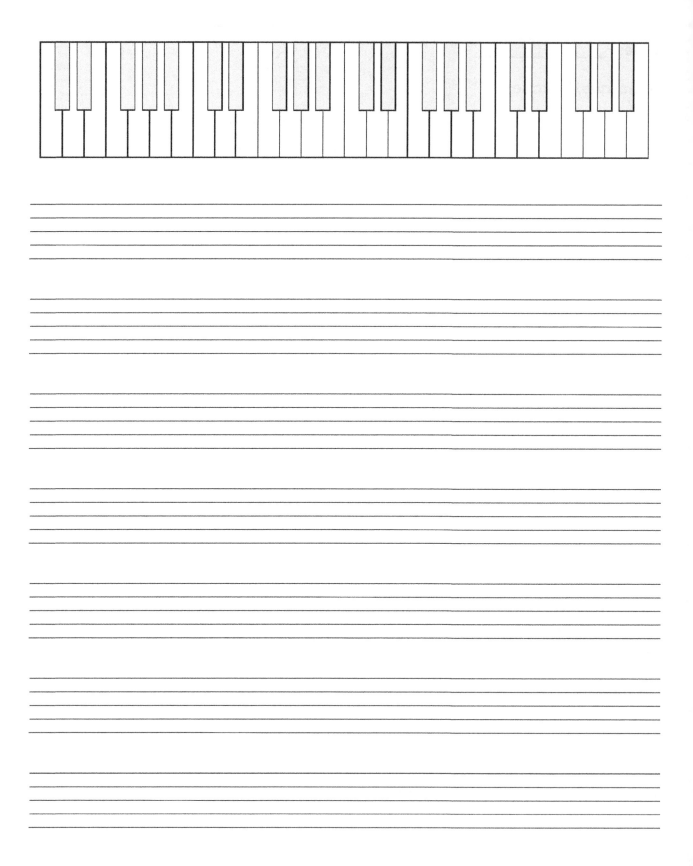

Date: _____

Technique/Exercises:

☆ ⬭

Repertoire:

Special Notes:

Practice Time Tracker:

Date:							
Minutes							
Initials:							

I have questions for the next lesson!

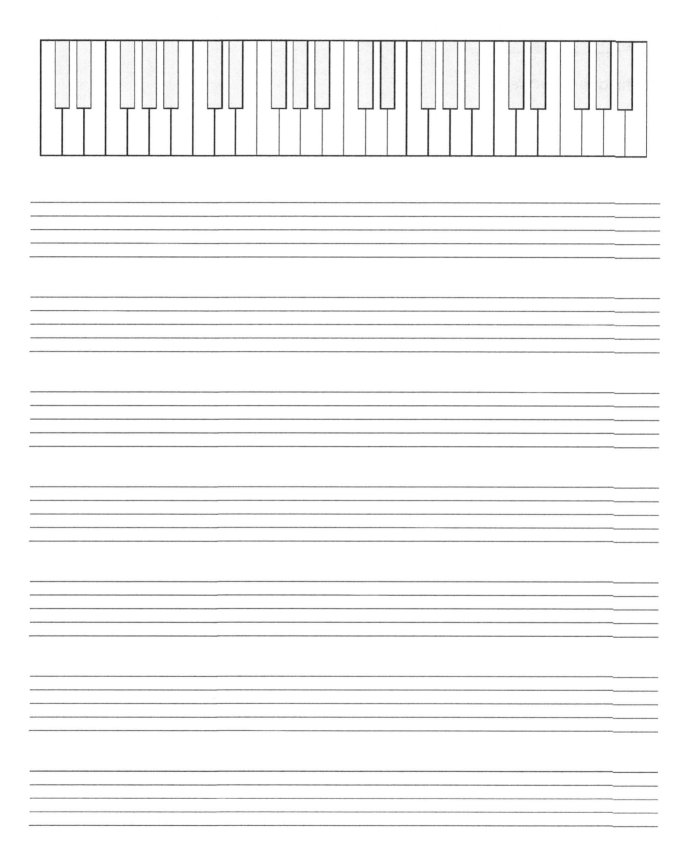

Date: _____

Technique/Exercises:

Repertoire:

Special Notes:

Practice Time Tracker:

Date:							
Minutes							
Initials:							

I have questions for the next lesson!

Date: _____

Technique/Exercises:

Repertoire:

Special Notes:

Practice Time Tracker:

Date:							
Minutes							
Initials:							

I have questions for the next lesson!

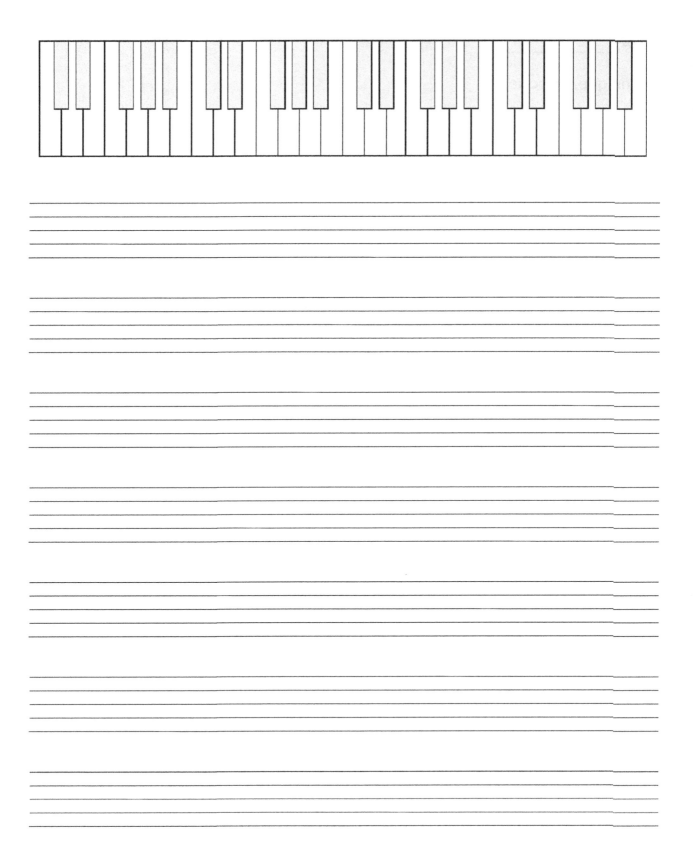

Date: _____

Technique/Exercises:

Repertoire:

Special Notes:

Practice Time Tracker:

Date:							
Minutes							
Initials:							

I have questions for the next lesson!

Date: _____

Technique/Exercises:

Repertoire:

Special Notes:

Practice Time Tracker:

Date:							
Minutes							
Initials:							

I have questions for the next lesson!

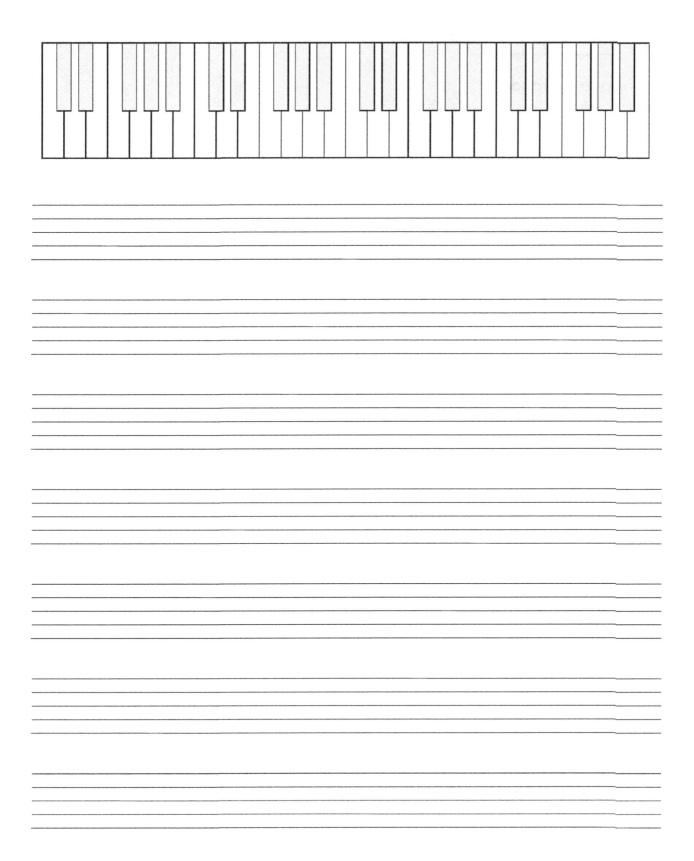

Date: _____

Technique/Exercises:

⭐

Repertoire:

Special Notes:

Practice Time Tracker:

Date:							
Minutes							
Initials:							

I have questions for the next lesson!

My Repertoire

My Repertoire (continued)

"*If I were not a physicist, I would probably be a musician. I often think in music. I live my daydreams in music. I see my life in terms of music.*"

~Albert Einstein

Made in the USA
Monee, IL
06 October 2022

15349135R10070